Energy Is
All Around

by Kristen Kunkel

 HOUGHTON MIFFLIN HARCOURT

forms of energy

heat

OPEN

light

sound

Energy causes changes.
Energy has many forms.
Energy comes from many places.

heat energy

Heat is a form of energy.
We feel heat with our sense of touch.
Heat can cook food.

heat energy

light energy

sound energy

Light is a form of energy.
We see light with our sense of sight.

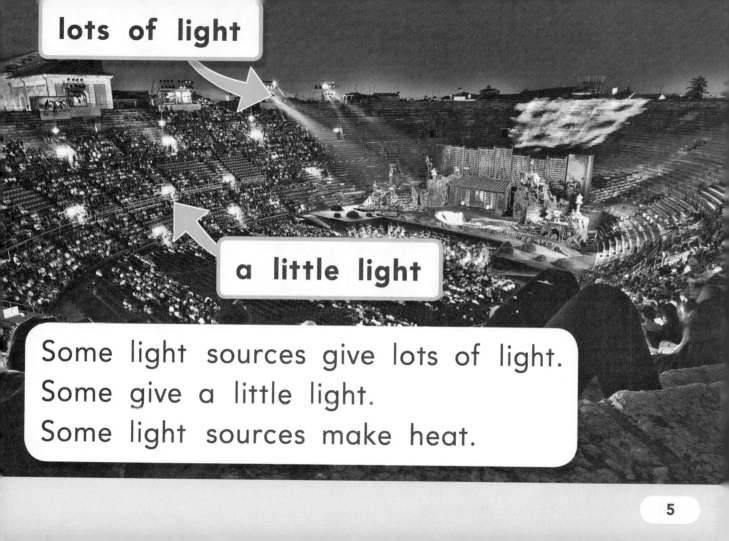

lots of light

a little light

Some light sources give lots of light.
Some give a little light.
Some light sources make heat.

sound energy

Sound is a form of energy.
Things vibrate and make sound.
We hear sound with our sense of hearing.

loud, high sound

Sounds can be loud or soft.
Sounds can be low or high.
There is energy all around us.

Draw an Energy Picture

Think of your favorite part of the day. Imagine where you are and what you do at that time. Use your senses to explore the forms of energy you see as you picture that time of day. Then draw a picture of your favorite part of the day. Label the forms of light, heat, and sound energy in your picture.

Write About Forms of Energy

Copy these sentences onto a sheet of paper. Write the form of energy that completes the first sentence. Then write your own sentence or draw a picture to tell how that form of energy helps you.

We see _____.

We feel _____.

We hear _____.

Vocabulary

energy	sight
hearing	sound
heat	sources
light	vibrate
sense	